Negotiation for Sales and Power: Negotiating Deals, Negotiation with Opponents, Negotiate Your Salary to Win

BENJAMIN TIDEAS

CONTENTS

INTRODUCTION

I want to thank you and congratulate you on reading this book, "Negotiation for Sales and Power: Negotiating Deals, Negotiation with Opponents, Negotiate Your Salary to Win".

This book contains proven steps and strategies on how to win the advantage in any negotiation you may encounter and how to excel in getting more out of every transaction in life – whether it is emotional, personal or financial. From the ancient times, the pattern of human life is such that one must have to go through negotiation. In addition, if you do not even know what negotiation is, that would make your life difficult to lead.

You spend most of your time negotiating without even knowing it. Negotiating with your toddler on what to eat, buying the latest model of laptop, or even just driving home with your partner and deciding which route to take. Negotiation is a part of your life. You cannot avoid it. One way or another you do it all the time. Sometimes it could be formal or sometimes informal. So, knowing how to get through negotiation should be working out for you throughout your life. As mentioned before, you do it all the time, but would it not be easier to grab your chances through negotiation when you know how to do one and how to persuade?

The need to negotiate can happen anytime, anywhere. You may not be involved in a hostage negotiation or making a one million dollar deal. However, it is very important that you arrive at a point where you and the other party both will win. This is very vital to keep your sanity, productiveness and peace of mind. Negotiation does not mean that every time only you would be the winning side. The real negotiation is when there is something for both parties. In a phrase, it's a 'win-win' situation. Of

1

course, your targets will be served in the first place; nevertheless, there shall always be something for the other party as well. Remember, it is a win-win situation. Think of the hostage crisis situation—what would be if the government representative were unwilling to talk to the other side holding guns in front of hundreds of innocents including women and children?

This book will make sure that you are ready and prepared to negotiate even on the roughest terrains and under the most daunting conditions.

Thanks again for reading this book, I hope you enjoy it.

Also, don't forget to grab your FREE Bonus book via the link at the end!

Now, let's get to it!

WHAT IS NEGOTIATION?

Negotiation is at the heart of any human interaction. Every time you are going to interact, there will be a negotiation that will take place—verbally or non-verbally, consciously or unconsciously. Whether talking to your kids, driving or doing your daily chores and errands—there will always be a negotiation. You will never get away from it. You can either do well or do poorly with negotiations.

The idea of negotiation is: a dialog between two or more parties (or persons) that are trying to reach a final solution or understanding without making it a huge compromise for any side. However, from many recent international events, we have observed that some of the negotiations are one sided. Thanks to the skill and experience of the winning parties, who not always possessed the required instruments or support to make it happen for them, still did it well and have managed to come out on top. This is why you need to tweak your negotiation skill. It is a never ending process, and you will learn it anew throughout your life. It will help you a great deal to be in a position to bring any situation to your favor anytime, anywhere.

Back to the definition, all the competing parties try to craft their interest in the first place to have the outcome in their favor. Nothing can stay out of the 'negotiation radar' whether it is a government institute, business or non-profit organization. Even in schools, hospitals, and courts negotiations takes place all the time. Even in relationships or other personal matters there is a role for negotiation. For example, think about divorce, marriage, and parenting. Would it be suitable for two sides in a divorce trying to reach a solution without starting a negotiation? No, it would be devastating. There is even a subject called 'Negotiation Theory.' Many countries or organizations tend to hire professional negotiators to appear as the more legit side in a negotiation. Some perfect and common example of negotiators are brokers, diplomats, and legislators.

However, you do not need to negotiate every minute and for everything in your life. We are only saying that people who are more conscious of the interactions they create, get more of what they really want to achieve in their life. There is no need to make every situation difficult by thinking there ought to be a negotiation. Not all situations ask for negotiation. So, you may have to be a little astute when it is the time to ring the bell. If you are thinking of negotiation all the way, you are wasting your time and energy.

Learning more about negotiation approaches and tools will be your vehicle to achieve greater skill and confidence that you can apply in your daily life. That is why you have to master the art of negotiation even if you are just another regular guy (or girl) on the road who is a vendor or trader. Negotiation skills would make your life a lot easier before approaching something, and it will give you the gist of integrity, self-reliance, aptitude and confidence before opening a new door each time in your lifetime.

Here are some key ideas to keep in mind in regards to negotiation:

Goals are supreme.

You obviously want to have achieved your goals at the end of every negotiation. Unfortunately, many people clearly do not attain their goals. Most of their actions are not according to their goals because they are focused on doing something else. They get angry at their relationship or at the store where they buy their favorite brands or stuff. They begin to attack the wrong people. Do not be like them. In a negotiation, you should be pursuing relationships, win-win situations, or interests because you know it is a very effective tool. Anything you do must bring you closer to achieving your goals. At the end of the day, only you are responsible for your action. If you are getting mad at someone for a simple reason, you are losing it all. You have lost it before even starting the game. Be cool, be responsible, and be gentle. Think about if you were on the other side of the river. Would it be the same? No, but that does not mean you should give up. It just tells you how to coat your wall so that the other side can start believing your perspective is the most beneficial. It is not like you are asking for the whole world. At a superstore, you might be competing with another person to get a product. Don't get physical or rude (supposing, you have a bad temper). You may present the reasons why you need this in the first place and who knows—the competitor could be willing to let it go if you suggest to him a substitute. Does this ring any bells?

It is about people.

You cannot convince a person unless you know what they have in their head – their needs, perceptions, and sensibilities; how they create commitments, and whether you can trust them or not. These bits of information are vital in order for you to know where you are going to start. You need to think that when you are going to negotiate, you must be thinking of yourself last at times. You have to imagine a role reversal – put yourself in the shoes of the person with whom you are negotiating. If you are to use your leverage and power without any finesse, it will cause retaliation and destroy relationships. The first mistake people commit during a negotiation, is thinking that they are the only person trying to win. This is a grave mistake. By doing so, you become a pusher but not a negotiator. This kind of mentality is well enough to end the last chance of sealing a deal. You need to listen and think. You need to give the other party some room, so he or she or they could share and let you know their concerns and logic. Let them talk and place a comparison sheet in your mind, fetch the reasons to continue to resolving.

Create emotional payments.

Whenever people are irrational, they are also emotional. If they are emotional, they usually cannot listen. If they do not listen, you cannot persuade them. This means everything that you say will be useless, especially if you have arguments that are only intended for reasonable or rational people. You have to tap the emotional psyche of a person with empathy. Apologize, if necessary, and offer them value with other angles that will surely persuade them to think more clearly. Never think of crossing the shadow line between emotion and professionalism. During a conversation making some erroneous comment is not abnormal, but what is wrong is the inability to admit mistakes. We have a tendency, not to take the blame for our mistakes. This is not good. Without going through the apology, your opponent has been given the 'OK' button to reach the emotional part. Also, once the button is pushed it would be very hard to make him, or her listen to even your most logical reasoning; it would only be a waste of time. So, handle any unprofessionalism and negativity intriguing part accordingly.

Every scenario must be treated differently.

In every negotiation, there is no one-size-fits-all solution for every situation. Even if you are going to negotiate with the same person at a different time, you should learn to analyze every inch of the situation. Keep in mind that there are many differences in every person that you meet. You should know how a person feels and thinks in order for you to know how you can better persuade them. If it were possible to have a fixed framework for setting up a general method for negotiation, it would be great. However, negotiation is not any regular concentration or subject that can be studied and followed with rules. It takes intelligence, manner, thinking, and decency to get to know what's going on in other's mind. Every person is a different individual. Even, when you met a person at different times, his or her attitude or mood could be totally different. You cannot afford to follow the same strategy every time you site for discussion. The pick is, you have got to get adapted to the situation with every new meeting. In the table of negotiation, there is no way to have the view that 'first expression is the last'. Being the considerate one is a part of the negotiation game. What you should be remembering is, the same is applicable to the other side. Thus, playing your cards accordingly and timely is indispensable.

Gradual is usually best.

Most people fail in negotiating because they are asking for too much. They create steps that are too big which will scare anyone. It will make the negotiation riskier, and it will only highlight the differences. When you are negotiating, try taking baby steps. Lead the person you are negotiating with, from the goals this person wants to attain to the picture that he or she sees in their head - or from the unfamiliar pictures to the familiar ones. Don't be impatient. Don't try to win the whole with a huge step. Following a pattern consisting favorable and small steps would prevent the other person from believing that you do not want to take away everything possible. In this way, he or she would never intend to give up the slightest things possible. Your job is not to persistently keep telling your side of the story like a mockingbird. Instead, consistently and gradually lead the other side from what they believe to what could happen if there were some changes in perspective. Also, try inserting a feasibility check in their head from their perspective. Think of it not so much as forcing the facts, but you are just bringing them to a realization.

Trade the things that hold less value to you.

Everyone values things unequally. First, you need to know what the involved parties care about and what they do not care about – tangible or intangible; small or big; emotional or rational; or even outside the deal. Then the next step is to trade off items in which the opposing party values highly for items that you do not. For instance, you are a manager who is doing the schedule of all the staffs involved in your store's operations. You are fixing the holiday schedule for everyone. Married people would prefer to have a day off during the holiday season because they want to spend time with their family. On the other hand, an unmarried staff member may love to work during the holidays because of the higher pay he or she will get. The two parties involved would both love to swap their schedule. You need to make use of the synapses of their lives in order to persuade the parties involved. In addition, you are also creating opportunities for both parties. In economics, there is a principle called opportunity cost. To put it simply, compare what benefits you are getting from a favorable outcome with the benefits that would be achieved by the other outcome you are giving up. When you accept a demand it does not necessarily mean you are losing, you could always get something else in return. Make sure the trade-off is in your favor that means you gain more than what you lose. If giving up smaller options may open up the way towards bigger doors, then what would you prefer?

Look for their standards.

What are their rules or policies? What will make them bend or make an exception to their policies? How do they make their decisions? Use the answers that you will get from the questions in order to get even more information that you can use. Identify their bad behavior whenever they are not consistent with their set of rules and policies. Did the hotel ever allow a late check-out? Do they prioritize high customer satisfaction? This strategy is perfect when you are dealing with hard bargainers. Setting up a standard for the other party could be crucial in winning the most out of something. Even a mighty negotiator would have some mistakes, weakness, and occasionally the lack of attention to detail. This is a great opportunity for you to realize what should make the other party break. What will enforce him to think differently? Be consistent with the way he is answering even in case of the basics, and never take something as enough. Use the answers as the key to raising some more questions—question that would get deeper with time and that would fetch more information than before. As deep as you go, you get to learn the person you are negotiating with, which should allow you some more room to be persuasive. In addition, of course, you are getting an image of how the other person thinks. What is his or her forte or indulgence? It becomes far easier to make him believe that your reasons are stronger than anything that could come out in the first place. This technique takes mastery, and once you attain it, should be easier for you to hold the 'Jack' even in the toughest table of negotiation.

Do not manipulate.

You should always be constructive and transparent and not manipulative. Do not ever deceive people – you do not have to. They will usually find out, and the payback will be long-term and negative to you. Always be yourself when you are negotiating. Do not pretend that you are nicer or tougher when you are not. The people you are interacting with will detect if you are deceiving them. Being real is more credible and often can act as your biggest asset. Pretending will never get you anything. The table of negotiation is not an act of drama. You may have been manipulating someone for a while to reach your goals and in the process you were successful for a while, but the result would never be in your favor. Also, once your manipulative face has been revealed, it would be very difficult to get them back in the negotiation with the previous respect and belief that they had for you. The whole negotiation will be a waste of time. So, being yourself is one of the basics. You cannot pretend what you are not. If you think you are getting something by being bossy or reflecting a winner from the beginning, you are being deceived by yourself. Never get into the table of negotiation with such mentality, be realistic and confident with your reasons; and must get to respect the others. Negotiation is nothing like a football game where there is always a loser and winner.

Communicate well.

Always send your obvious vision: learn to communicate. Most negotiations that fail are due to bad communication or none at all. You should not walk away from any negotiation unless you want to end the negotiation, a resolution is reached, or all parties involved agreed to take a break. If you are not communicating, it means you are not getting the needed information. The best negotiators will always state the real situation such as, "You know what? It seems that we are not getting along very well – how can we improve that?" Being in a convenient position will not assure that you are going to return home with your hands full. You have to work for it. So keep up the communication channels flexible, friendly, and cordial throughout the discussion. When there are communication gaps, the negotiation is doomed to be broken anytime. Maintain courtesy and mutual respect but don't get too formal. It is not a show of how well behaved or educated you are, it is a real deal that takes you to know every possible piece of information in order to stand out. You should not be waiting for the other party to break the ice when there is an impasse. Your smartness is, frankly speaking, what is going wrong and what should be done regarding that. This, in reality, sets your position higher than the party on the other side of the table.

Identify the underlying issue.

Search for the real concern and grab it as an opportunity. Most people find it very difficult to mention the underlying and real problems. Ask yourself, "What are the real reasons that prevent me from achieving my goals?" In order for you to find out the real problem, you need to find out what is causing the other party to act the way he or she is acting. Probing is an excellent tool to use until you find what you are looking for. You need to get into their shoes and understand their perspective. Each moment in a negotiation is valuable. A moment wasted means an opportunity gone. Moreover, there are situations when it needs to be quick, or the consequences could be grave. Sometimes side talks are required to keep a natural flow in any negotiation, but don't spend all time in it. Stay firm with your goal. Always keep in mind whatever concern is raised, you cannot afford to be derailed from the original process. If, often, you realize that the discussion is not on the right path, ask yourself over and over: why I am here in the first place? Get back to the primary concern and try reaching a solution.

Learn to embrace differences.

Most people treat differences as uncomfortable, risky, worst case, and annoying, but if you think about it, being different is often better, more creative, and more profitable. It can lead to more ideas, more perceptions, additional options, better results and better negotiations. The inability to admit differences is the other name of incapability in negotiation. You cannot expect everything to be the way you see it. When there is no difference or different opinion, the outcome is rigid, and there is no way to experience other options in hand that could make the negotiation more effective. You have got to listen and think of what the other side is going through, even if it contradicts your thinking. If a negotiation was to be one sided then what is the need of sitting together in the first place? Give some room and get some. Who knows, what the other side has to say might come up with something that not only preserves his or her interest, but yours as well.

Have a plan.

Prepare and create a list of strategies – a battle plan. The strategies mentioned above are the beginning of your list. Your list is like your smorgasbord where you can choose and utilize the items you need in order to achieve what you want. This is the last but not least step before sitting at the table of negotiation. No matter how strong position you are holding you have got to be well organized. Take a piece of paper and write down the sequence what comes after what, what would be the points that ask for the majority of attentions, and when and where to use one or more strategies. A good plan means you are in a point of advantage even before starting to negotiate. As you go forward, this strategic planning shall be proven valuable in winning small phases of negotiation. So never think of planning as a minor part of the game!

COMMUNICATION AND PERCEPTION

Look at the picture below the end of this paragraph. What do you see? You might answer that it is a black dot, or it is a black circle. This simple question can draw many different answers. Heck, a medical student might answer that it is "streptococcus".

The primary reason negotiations fail, is due to communication failure. The greatest reason for communication failure is misconception. Just ask two persons to look at a single picture at the same time. They will look at it differently in at least some way every time.

What causes the various perceptions of different people? First, everyone is a unique individual. Some things may be interesting for some people that might not be interesting for others. Everyone has their set of values and emotional make-ups. You have been influenced as well by other people while growing up or even as you grow old. You observe and experience different things, and collect abundant information, which you may either utilize or simply ignore if it does not fit your needs.

As one's taste does not match another's, we tend to see the difference as something odd and vice versa. Differences project light on something that you are unable to think of or never intended to. With every difference, there comes an idea. More or less for everyone it is quite difficult to listen to other's thinking about the same matter. You may think, only and only, your thought is the one fitting answer to something critical. Ok, set up your mind—at least you would listen to what others have to say. Once you have listened carefully then why don't compare it with yours? Alternatively, if they still seem not applicable or realizable, create some counter production to establish why yours are going to work in the first place. It would make your points even stronger and rational.

In negotiations, you usually selectively collect evidence that will support your personal insights, opinions or views. You also selectively recall things. Your memories always impress color onto your perceptions. However, it is also important to use your sense, agility, and intuition. It cannot be done under a set of strict rules. Use your knowledge - sometimes out of a book, sometimes out of ordinary experience - this is what makes the difference.

As you can see, there are plenty of key reasons as to why people have conflicts.

THE PERCEPTION GAP

There are some people who will treat the perceptions of other people as incorrect. Also, if other people do not see their point of view, they will brand these people as stubborn or unreasonable. There is no room for stubbornness. The one and only outcome of stubbornness is 'futile'.

However, that is not the biggest problem. Most of the time, the problem is what you hold so dearly and firmly might not be applicable or visible to other people. For others, it does not even exist, or at minimum, it is not important to them. Why would someone put down an idea that doesn't even register on a list for them? You see a point from an angle, but as the angle changes the point may seem different—or, it may not even look like a point at all.

It does not mean that you ought to give up your perspective. In order for you to persuade someone with different perceptions, you may need to begin making your ideas, facts, perceptions and thoughts visible to them. Make them see what they do not see, but the precondition is to know why they do not see or don't want to see. It would be easier that way. Why your perception stands along among the crowd should make a total difference, with a nicer impact.

Here is a clear example of this scenario: In the marketing department, the employees have different definitions of the term "marketing." They have been using the term every day, and yet they are not on the same page. Some define it as a close relation to sales; some define it as a strategy. With this situation, they have different perceptions such as on how they do and approach their jobs, deal with their customers, and spend the company's resources. For the sake of the company, there need to be a common goal and how could it be set when no department is on the same page? Is it so tough? We do not think so. There will be some commonness even in each different definition, the gist of which could be used effectively to set up the ultimate way to define marketing without being opposed.

Experienced lawyers who are negotiating complex contracts know that they need to include clear definitions of terms that will be used in the agreement. They realize that even a simple word will be subject to various interpretations. If the different parties involved in the negotiation have a different understanding of specific terms, the whole process of agreement will be at risk because there is no meeting of the minds.

In the last example it is more severe than the marketing side of a company, so a resolution must be found.

CLOSING THE PERCEPTION GAP

Now, how do you solve the problems of perception and miscommunication? You should realize first that these problems and challenges will take place everywhere and pretty much every time. Then, your next question may be, "What is the language being used?" Both parties should mean the same thing by getting on the same page. The impact of a perception gap is wider than that you could have imagined. In every event of life, you are going to face it. There is no way to skip it. So the other feasible way is to face it with full preparation—that is reducing the gap as much as possible—so that conflicts may not take place.

For instance, you are going to tell your niece a story. You might say, "Ok, I will be telling you a story." Then your niece says, "No, I want two stories." For you, you intended to tell one long story. On the other hand, your niece is thinking of a story that is short. You both wanted to have the same amount of story time, but each of you thought the other was getting the better end of the bargain – all due to the perception of language.

When you are having conflicts with someone, ask yourself the following:

a. What do I perceive?
b. What do they perceive?
c. Is there a gap between myself and the other party?
d. If yes, what is it?
e. If so, how to resolve it?

You have already done this in an unstructured way many times in your life. Now that you are aware make it a point that you ask these specific questions yourself. This also means that you need to try to understand all the biases of the parties involved in the negotiation. You have to try your hardest to articulate their different perceptions and then you need to explain yours. Now that you are learning them like rules, it should be easier for you to proceed.

Consider these two statements:

a. "I am going to Paris. Where are you going?"
b. "Where are you going? I am going to Paris."

These two sentences have the same words but in a different order. You will probably hear most of the time statement number two. Asking someone first about their perception shows that you value them. As a result, they will be much more interested in whatever you want to say next. This trick is important in order to show you contain enough respect for the other party and as a result you can expect the same. When you show someone that there is no lacking in your perceived credibility about him or her, you will be treated the same way. Thus goes the old saying, "Respect in order to get respect."

In the above examples, it is very vital that you should also remember not to be interrupting someone speaking or saying what they want to say. Most of the time, when a person is being interrupted while saying their piece or giving their insights, they will be annoyed or angry with you. This is a bad habit to interrupt someone while he or she is speaking. By interrupting when someone is speaking, you are destroying the natural flow of that person. Additionally, the person has every right to be mad at you. It also bears a degree of disrespect. When it comes to your turn, the other party usually will not hesitate to do the same.

Here are examples of what usually happens during negotiations:

"My offer is $400,000 for this house that is based on the market conditions right now."

"Currently, the housing prices are on a downtrend. This is the perfect time to sell your house."

If you have been using the two examples above as your starting point, it is like you are walking in the dark. You need to understand how the parties picture something in their heads. Know how they perceive and feel the world. Know how they view you. You need to try heart and soul to be in their mind—the way they think, the way they want to proceed, the way they value you. In this way, you could be expecting what should come next.

Instead, try something more like this, "Hello. This is such a wonderful house that you have. How long have you been in this place?"

Remember that you should be saying and explaining your perceptions last. You need to learn first their perceptions. One excellent way of understanding the party's or the person's perception is through asking questions and probing. In every negotiation, questions are more powerful than giving statements. Questions have had the capability to reveal everything that has not been exposed yet. With proper questioning, the other side will be willing to disclose something that wasn't exposed at other times, or that might not come out naturally. Also, the person you are negotiating with will get the 'to go' ticket to reflect his or her perception. This would make negotiation easier as you are learning what is expected of you and what is not. You may bring down the other side's concerns under the same microscope and dissect them before you throw your perception. This will make your perception harder to be denied by the other party.

Any statement will commit you to anything that you say. It will not get you any information. However, if you are asking questions, you are not committing yourself to anything. You will get the information you need eventually, and it will allow you to proceed with things as you wish. When you are making statements, rather than questioning, you may be making pledges that could not be possible for you to keep in the end. So the statement game is a risky one. What you should do is, asking for all the possible facts to get ready for the sequences of the negotiation. This way, the negotiation could move forward in time.

In a negotiation, you should be asking questions often. It will certainly help you find out if the parties involved are interested in communicating with you in the first place. Try to turn your statements into questions. Say, "Do you think it is fair?" instead of "This is not fair." Ask your daughter, "Could you tell me why you are not doing your homework?" instead of, "Go and do your homework." Keep questioning all the time to be sure that the other party is really into the negotiation and not just randomly answering your questions to get rid of you. Even when a statement is inevitable, you are always free to turn it into a question. This way the involved parties believe they have options. This is a realistic approach to negotiation. There is no benefit to the discussion if the parties involved believe you are only interested in listening to what you think as right and nothing more than that. Questioning is also the best way to keep up the curiosity level.

Asking questions will encourage the parties involved to participate in the conversation. You have better chances of getting valuable information this way. However, the negotiation will not be over after you get an answer to your question. It would end when you decided it should.

How to Bridge the Communication Gap

One of the main reasons for miscommunication that often leads to failed deals and conflicts in negotiation is that you assume the specific pictures and knowledge that is in the mind of the other party. However, those perceptions and knowledge are usually not there since your assumptions are based on your experiences and your biases. You need to begin from the start and go through step-by-step, following their pace and not yours if you want to persuade them. Negotiation is not something like creating a hypothesis, and then proceeding based on that without assessing it first. If you are unable or unwilling to find out what is going on in the involved parties' mind you must not go ahead just with what you think of as their way of thinking.

Here are the key concepts of effective communication:
- Always communicate
- Learn to ask questions and listen
- Give value: do not blame anyone
- Make it a habit to summarize information
- Do role shifting
- Be dispassionate, cool and calm
- Be firm without ruining the relationship
- Articulate your goals
- Search for signals
- Discuss differences
- Search for clues on how they make commitments
- Always consult before making decisions
- Concentrate only on what you can control
- It is a no-no to debate who is right or wrong

STANDARDS AND POLICIES

One of the greatest tools in negotiation that most people do not think about is using the other person's policies and standards in life. Standards are very effective, especially with hard bargainers. Standards are the criterions that the other party believes and thinks to be fair.

One byproduct of standardization is that it holds a stigma for what has been done one way all along. The main theme of standard practice is to make the participating counterpart to a fixed way because of the only reason: it is the settled policy. Most of the time, this tactic works magnificently as it is proven to be the safest approach. The most common example of this is the standard contract,—where the signing party, in general, preserves the idea that the contract is non-changeable. It is possible to get the best outcome simply by asking: how standard a contract is or its magnitude.

For example, Richie is planning to rent some new office space. The renter asks Richie to sign an agreement called 'Standard Commercial Lease,' which is to be signed in two places. But what if Richie is not willing to sign the paper without being assured of every detail first? He can follow the salami approach—that is turning a slice after slice and asking what's in it. In words that is—the standardization may be applicable for some of the terms but not for all. Alternatively, he could offer to the renter that he would sign the agreement without any further question, but there has to be a trade-off. For example, he can ask for a cut in the first month's rent. Alternatively, he could demand some changes in the agreement that serve his interest in the first place. If the renter exposes his reluctance even after such negotiation, you could stop questioning and get going to other places that suit you. I call this last one the "these boots were made for walking" policy, and it is necessary when there is no other way out.

Have you used or encountered this tactic in your negotiations? If so, how'd it go?

Imploring the standards of the other party is very important because you are living in an uncertain and unfair world. Companies and people tend to violate their own policies and standards. They often create service promises and then break them. The situation could be such that the party you are negotiating with is talking about simplicity, but when it comes to applying them, some points or terms appear to be not working.

Perhaps you order something from an online store, and they do not deliver as promised. It could be that they had promised you something extravagant, saying: "Everything is perfect. You deserve the best." They promised excellent service, but you were treated poorly. What they did was generalizing matter rather than going through the details. You always rely on what they have promised and yet do not feel sorry for their shortcomings, and this can drive you crazy. Now, what you can do is: use their policies and standards in order to get what you want.

How would that work? It is an essential principle of human psychology that a person hates to contradict himself or herself. Almost every person believes only what they think is real, and others cannot see it in the right way. This means if you give a person the option to choose between:

a. Being consistent with what they have promised previously, while staying consistent with what they believe as good standards, or...
b. Contradicting their previous word (even though they now believe it to be truer) and relaxing on their standards...

That person will most likely strive harder to stay consistent with their first declaration of their standards. Obviously, you need to keep in mind that there is no tool that will always work effectively. Also, you cannot expect every individual to follow the same tendency every time. However, this is generally how it works.

Here is a concrete example of using standards to win in a negotiation - the scenario is this: you received a damaged dress after sending it to the dry cleaner's shop. "Is it your company policy to send the dress back to your customer with a torn hemline and fewer buttons than it arrived with?" In asking this question, you are utilizing standards. This might sound aggressive to you, but you are merely asking them a question regarding their standards. You may re-word it any way you wish, however, the principle is clear – it is not the job of the dry cleaner shop to damage the hemline and lose any of the buttons on your gown. This is clearly drawing a line between what is legit and what is not for the cleaning service,—that they do not have the right to implement any change in the cloth intentionally or accidently.

Here is another example: you may say to your spouse or partner, "Honey, the last five movies we have watched were titles that you wanted to watch. Isn't it my turn to choose a movie?" Again, feel free to use different words. But what you are doing here is asking your partner if he or she simply believes that the right in choosing a movie to watch should be fairly shared between you and your partner. Their standards will answer in the affirmative. This kind of asking is legalizing your thought of fair share of the right to pick a movie in a relationship, which is no way official! However, you can see the standard and policy are working here with the same vigor. This is an unwritten standard that both the partners get the equal share in decision-making. For a healthy relationship, both partners are expected to be affirmative in a way or another.

One of the advantages of using the policies and standards of a person is that it is a transparent procedure. You are not manipulating anyone. You can bluntly say to the other party what you are doing. If the other party asks you, "Are you imploring policies and standards on me?" Answer the question with, "Yes, of course. What is wrong with utilizing your well-considered standards and criteria as your basis for your decisions?"

Setting Standards and Policies

Before any negotiation happens, you need to set your standards and policies. Most people will put values on the general rule at the beginning of any procedure. If you wait, and then try to set standards and policies later on once it has benefited you, the other party will think that you are manipulating them, and you are taking advantage of the scenario.

Your Competitive Attitude

Competitive negotiation is another valuable concept, along with staying focused on the present goal instead of being distracted by the big picture. Do not be distracted with losing or winning, what happened a while ago, an unfair game, what might happen later or whatever emotions you have at the moment. Instead, concentrate and execute: "What are the goals that I want to attain right now? What are the policies and standards that I should use? What are the needs of the different parties involved? Who is the ultimate decision maker in the company?"

Before negotiating, you are going to prepare and strategize. You will concentrate and make your strategy happen. If you see a problem, you may need to rest and take a break. You may need to re-evaluate your strategy and make the necessary adjustments. Then, you can go back to negotiating and execute your strategies more effectively.

HOW DO WE NEGOTIATE?

Now that you have learned all the concepts that you need for successful negotiation; you are probably asking, "What am I going to do with all of these?"

Attitude: Start with your attitude. If you are going to be distracted, afraid and nervous, you will only do poorly. A high level of confidence is vital. Remember, the other party will see and feel if you are nervous.

Preparation: Perhaps the biggest factor, to having a successful negotiation, is coming well-prepared. The more you prepare yourself, the more you are confident and less nervous. You will not be worrying yourself about the things that you do not know.

When and where to conduct the negotiation: It does not matter as long as you can negotiate and feel comfortable about the location. In case the other party will create things that will make you uncomfortable, say "I am not yet ready to negotiate" or "It is making me uncomfortable."

Get to know each party: An informal way of getting to know each other is totally fine. No incantations or dance steps needed. A simple, "Hi," or "Hey, what's up?" will do in most situations. Give compliments to the other party. Find a common interest that you both like. Just make sure that you mean it – making efforts in knowing the person. Conducting small talk is very crucial in negotiations. It should be called big talk. It creates human connections that are obviously critical.

Getting started: Even in a small negotiation, you should know, specifically, what you have got there to talk about in the first place. That means the subject matter that will be covered and in what chronological order. You have to get an agenda that will happen which was agreed upon by both parties. This is needed in order to have something to get back to in case all parties involved lose track of what is going on.

The dynamics of negotiation: Keep in mind that, during the negotiation, you have to discuss the perceptions of the other party every time you are confronting a new issue. Through your role shifting and preparation before the negotiation, you should be equipped with concepts that you can share. If you are going to persuade them, start with their perceptions. If you are caught off guard or surprised, or if there are disagreements, take a break.

How to treat each party involved in the negotiation: It is inadvisable to treat other parties with threats, sarcasms, or insults. Failing to communicate will just lead you to unresolved issues or worse, with greater problems. You need to use words properly. For instance, instead of saying, "We do not trust you" say, "Why don't we start trusting each other?"

Extreme offers: Forget about extreme offers. It will only kill your deals. Plus, the other party will only feel insulted. It will also put your credibility at risk. Why? In case you give extreme offers and then immediately back off, then the other party will think that you are just taking advantage of them, and mistrust will emerge.

Now that you know all these, it is still not enough. You have to actually do it – make it happen! You are ready. So, get out of your shell and go get more of what you deserve.

SECRETS TO PLAYING THE NEGOTIATION GAME

Rule #1: Don't be so desperate for a deal. It is impossible to get something that you have set as a must get for you. From the moment the other side notices that you would not like anything but a win, they will make you pay for it, and the price will be nothing less than the highest. Do you know? In any negotiation, the losing side is always the one that desperately seeks for the bargain. The aim should be making the other side realize that they need it more than you do, and you would not hesitate to leave the table straightaway unless they afforded a better deal.

Rule #2: Give up something only when you are set to get something in return. Never discount the least important thing without being ensured you are getting some in return. I would not wonder if you were willing to give up something just for the sake of presenting something, which would draw your image as positive, frank, and friendly. You might be thinking, "what harm is in it when the thing you are losing bears no importance to your cause?" But the math is different at the table of negotiation. Negotiators are tricky people and believe in diplomacy no less than an ambassador. Unless you are very lucky, they will take it for granted and assume you are weak. Additionally, they will get back to rule #1, thinking you want to get the deal at any cost. They will make it even harder for you by asking for larger flexibilities and always be keeping you under pressure. Give respect and expect the same with every offer you make, with this they will have the feeling that nothing is for free, and they have got to work for it. It will also win you some level of respect.

Rule #3: Never take a deal that makes lack of sense. Don't be hasty when you are on the brink of getting a deal. Getting a deal is not anything until you can see it in introspective. If the other party is asking for something that will leave you with nothing, let them know and ask for equivalent compensation that would keep your concerns satisfied as well. Here you are rational, and trying to be at a level that will fill in the gaps that are resultant of giving up the 'Jack'.

Rule #4: Negotiation is no different than any regular game. As like as any game, there must be an ending. If all the parties have the goodwill to reach a resolution, it should not take forever to reach a deal. Indeed, the longer it takes, the lesser the chance of getting a deal it becomes. When you've achieved your main goals in a deal then why waste time in worthless mushrooms? Get the deal done and don't look back.

BRIDGING A LANGUAGE/SOCIAL GAP

In North America, there can be a tendency to follow the 'my way or the highway' approach. Many Americans believe that since immigrants are coming to their land and making a living, they should pursue the American way of life more than anyone else. Many first-generation Americans of a foreign descendant stick with their value and norms while they are also living the American dream. So, it is not reasonable to expect them to forget their roots once and for all.

So, we need to accept the cultural differences in order to restrict the gap from widening. Accordingly, many foreigners are not completely aware of the customs of this region. Take, for example, an incident, where some newly immigrated people are making racist gestures to each other. They might not have thought that this kind of gestures could be considered performing some kind of taboo! Thus, it is crucial to have the consciousness that what you are thinking is strange could be a common thing for the other party. While negotiating, you have to make sure these differences do not take over the place of the main proposition. Mutual respect and understandings are necessary for this.

Though called as the universal language, English is hard to learn for the people who have never been into this language, especially for immigrants. When people struggle to speak English, they try the same broken words with a louder voice. That does not help either. Speaking simpler sentences is what can make it count. While speaking to the other party, you need to keep these facts in mind and behave accordingly. If the other party has a hard time understanding every word you say, you should consider speaking slowly in simple sentences—and if required, don't forget to repeat them.

READING BODY LANGUAGE

Body languages are a great reflector of our success and happiness and sorrow. All your preparation will be in vain if you cannot even understand the posters of the party with whom you are negotiating. There are some common signs or indicators that can be useful:

Identifying Baseline: The idea is to observe people when they are not in a tensed situation. In other word—they are not under pressure. During informal chit-chat try asking some questions, to the answers of which you are already familiar. See if they are answering in a calm, patient, honest, and relaxed manner. Identifying baseline is the first thing to do as it makes interpreting body language easier throughout the negotiation.

Look for the Gesture Clusters: Gesture clusters are hidden in clues like actions, postures, and other nonverbal communication—all of which are to direct that a particular view is being emphasized. So, during conversation, you cannot afford to miss those nonverbal clues. Also, look for disagreement action, tension signs, and engagement actions.

- **Engagement Actions**: Leaning forward, eye contact, head nods— these are the indicator of growing interest and agreement.
- **Disagreement Actions**: Looking away, frowning, leaning back are all indicators of annoyance, suspicion, disinterest, and boredom.

Tension Cues: Some signs that clearly dictate lack of satisfaction and a growing level of discomfort are—firmly crossed ankles, raising vocal tone, and face touching.

HANDLING DIFFICULT OR STRESSFUL SITUATIONS IN NEGOTIATION

A balance must be required between the sensitiveness and communication, especially when the situation is difficult. The required skills to be in this balancing position maybe are contradicting, as it will take you to be firm and gentle at the same time. To handle a situation that is either difficult or stressful, the necessary skill sets are:

Be Assertive: While setting up communication you need to be as assertive as possible. Unless it takes you to, don't back up your mind-to-mind conversation.

Be Emphatic: Try thinking of how you would feel if you were on the other side of the table listening to the same reasoning you have been putting on. Allow the involved parties to think thoroughly and ask some questions.

Certain Amount of Negotiation: This is a prerequisite to handling any difficult situation in a negotiation. Looking forward to a win-win situation should be preferred where there will be something for all the parties.

Use Verbal and Nonverbal Language: Must avoid any jargon or ambiguous manner. Always make eye contact while speaking and stay relaxed whether you are sitting or standing. Never even think of using body language or language that seems offensive.

Listen Carefully: When we feel stressed it becomes harder for us to listen with the same amount of attention as before. You have got to listen to others' point of views, opinions, and feelings about a certain matter.

Stay Calm: Conversation becomes more natural and meaningful when we are calm and positive. If you are feeling the heat, try taking some long breath. Others are likely to be calm when you are calm yourself. Never get deviated from your original mission, stay focused. If required, read it out in your mind like homework.

SALARY NEGOTIATION

Negotiating your salary all comes down to mindset and preparation - the latter being the most important. If you are confident of your abilities and what you have to offer the company you're negotiating with, you'll do well. If you come to the meeting more prepared than your opponent, manager or recruiter, (or competing applicant) you will put yourself in a position to win.

There are two instances in which you may find yourself in a salary negotiation. You could say three, but I consider vying for a freelance job or attempting a new employed position to be a very similar process. The other instance would be if you already work within a company and wish to negotiate a raise. They both, of course, have similar methods.

It's all about VALUE

The main point I want to get across in this section is to reverse the way you think about this process as compared to how most people view it. Most people go into a salary discussion thinking only about what they are worth, how they are underpaid, what the company owes them or how they're going to try to get everything that's coming to them. But I would like to challenge you to think much more about what you can offer to the employer, manager or entrepreneur in terms of value. Because think of it from his chair, what exactly is going to be the best reason for paying the person across from you more money? It's not how well he convinces you that you should part with more budget. It is based on how much value that particular individual is going to provide. You see, managers and companies usually don't mind paying a premium price for high value. But that value does not come from begging or demanding on the part of the person requesting salary.

If you get into this mindset of, "How can I provide this company more value than they are expecting and more value than any other applicant?" you will be unstoppable in a salary negotiation. The only thing left to do is to walk that walk with untouchable preparation. Never make salary an early point of discussion, but when the time comes to talk numbers, you want to be the most prepared person they've ever sat across from.

Get Prepared

The first step in being prepared is to do some comparable research. If you are looking for employment or a raise, go to salary.com and spend some time nailing down what your position is worth in your industry. Your prospective employer will have a good idea, and it's smart to be familiar with it yourself. (Bonus points if you end up educating him/her about these numbers) If you are looking for freelance work, search online at places like elance.com and odesk.com as well as others. Create an account as if you were looking to hire a freelancer yourself. Look for the skills that you are looking to provide yourself, and see what the market offers. You'll see a wide range, but you'll get a feel for that value. Don't be eager to look at the lowest numbers necessarily. You aren't the Wal-Mart of employees, and you don't sell yourself on price because if you do, someone will undercut you. Besides, weren't we talking about raising your salary here?

Break down the job posting that you are looking to apply for or have an interview lined up on. Look at all of the tasks or areas of expertise the company or hiring party is looking for. Then go one step further on them: brainstorm how those tasks would spill into other areas or how they might have advanced versions or next steps. Create a quick document with that list and spell out how and why you're qualified for each of them, why you can overcome experience lack and especially how you can exceed the job post's requirements. If you are looking for an existing raise, plot out all of the ways that you've helped the company over the past three months that may or may not be on your manager's radar. Sometimes just bringing these points to light will spur a manager to say, "You know, you're right - you do deserve more compensation."

I mean, how would you feel if you were a hiring manager who needed a certain five tasks completed, but while interviewing you found someone who proved they not only could accomplish all of them, but the next level tasks as well? You would feel like you just hit the bonus jackpot! Less training you have to do and innovative next steps are always music to a manager's ears. Be that someone.

Next, do some research on the company you're applying to be a part of. Or, if you already work there, make a list of things that could use some improvement in the company. Heck, if you need to, you can ask an entrepreneur where they think their weak links are at and what areas they'd like to shore up. We're making a list of things that could be fixed, and then you're going to write a little blurb about how you would plan to solve them. This is going to accomplish a few things.

You're probably going to hit on a couple points that are introspective of the job, and managers love to see that you're thinking ahead.

You'll likely list a couple things that manager hadn't thought about yet and give them a little 'ahh good point' moment.

You will bring up things that he knows are problems that he/she does not want to address. Did I just find someone who can take that off my plate? Excellent.

Write a sentence each that shows you understand the problem, 2-3 ideas on how it could be improved, and tests that would demonstrate their progress. To be honest, it doesn't even matter if your ideas work or not - it's the initiative here that is jacking up that value/salary meter.

If you are a current employee looking for a raise, your job is even easier. You already know the internal issues that could be improved where you work, and you've undoubtedly brainstormed ways to improve them. Make this list the same way described above and go in with (metaphorical) guns blazing!

The Right Stuff

So, now that you have done your diligent research for your interviews, (not every single position you apply for - just the ones that reach stage 2) it's time to put it all together and get ready to kick some butt. Put together your materials that you've gathered thus far including:

Research you've gathered from salary.com or freelance sites that demonstrate your applicable range

Your rendition of the job post's tasks, next-level tasks and why you're qualified and ready to go above and beyond.

A qualitative write-up that lists issues within the company that could be improved and your suggestions on how to improve them. (avoid anything that is embarrassing to the company - use standard issues every company might face that they deal with specifically)

Read over this small set of documents (3-4 pages max) to give yourself the confidence you should have going into a salary negotiation. After all, if you're not confident about what you bring to the table (literally and figuratively) your 'opponent' isn't going to give you much favor - and why should they? They're looking for max value!

After reading this printed document, you should have instilled a LOT of confidence in yourself. After all, you are what this company/entrepreneur needs to take their business to the next level. And I promise you, that is their primary concern - taking their business to the next level, not 'paying each employee what they want'. If you are going to provide value at a level that ensures their business moves toward the next level, they'll pay a fair and handsome rate, period.

Have confidence in your skill and your preparation. If you use the information above and you do not get the salary you deserve, then that company likely is one of the few that hires strictly on price, and they just made a mistake. Lucky for you, they're not the last stop. A valuable asset like yourself that can articulate your value to a hiring manager will not need to look long before a smart company snatches your services up and pays fairly to do so. Keep going, and know that you will soon get what you're worth using these techniques!

CONCLUSION

I want to personally Thank You again for reading this book!

I sincerely hope the information contained will help you to achieve more in life going forward by giving you the upper hand in all of your negotiating endeavors. With practice, you will become keen to negotiate in places others fail to recognize the opportunity, thus improving your skills at negotiation even further.

The next step is to put into practice the methods and employ the strategies we've discussed here to begin taking each of your negotiating opportunities to the next level!

Finally, if you enjoyed this book, please take the time to share your thoughts and post a positive review on Amazon. I would greatly appreciate your support!

Thank you and good luck!

Benjamin Tideas

ADDITIONAL RESOURCES

Please point your web browser to
www.plaid-enterprises.com/negotiate
for more Negotiation resources, my full bibliography and to grab your
FREE book!

www.ingramcontent.com/pod-product-compliance
Lightning Source LLC
Chambersburg PA
CBHW071018180526
45168CB00003B/1474